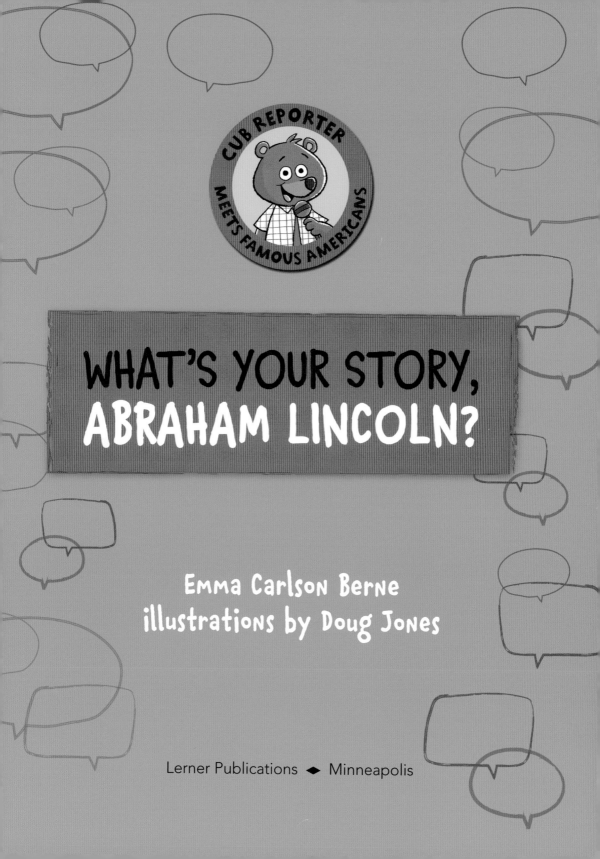

CUB REPORTER
MEETS FAMOUS AMERICANS

WHAT'S YOUR STORY, ABRAHAM LINCOLN?

Emma Carlson Berne
illustrations by Doug Jones

Lerner Publications ◆ Minneapolis

Note to readers, parents, and educators:
This book includes an interview of a famous American. While the words this person speaks are not his actual words, all the information in the book is true and has been carefully researched.

Lerner Publications Company
A division of Lerner Publishing Group, Inc.
241 First Avenue North
Minneapolis, MN 55401 USA

For reading levels and more information, look up this title at www.lernerbooks.com.

Main body text set in Avenir LT Pro 45 Book 15/21. Typeface provided by Linotype AG.

Library of Congress Cataloging-in-Publication Data

Berne, Emma Carlson.
  What's your story, Abraham Lincoln? / by Emma Carlson Berne.
    pages cm. — (Cub reporter meets famous Americans)
  ISBN 978-1-4677-7969-2 (lb : alk. paper) — ISBN 978-1-4677-8541-9 (pb : alk. paper) — ISBN 978-1-4677-8542-6 (eb pdf)
    1. Lincoln, Abraham, 1809–1865—Juvenile literature. 2. Presidents—United States—Biography—Juvenile literature. I. Title.
E457.905.B48 2016
973.7092—dc23 [B]   2015001955

Manufactured in the United States of America
1 – VP – 7/15/15

Table of Contents

Hi, everyone! Today, I'm interviewing a very important person. His name is Abraham Lincoln. Abe, what makes you special? Can you tell us a little about yourself?

Abe says: I'd love to tell you about myself! I was the president of the United States from 1861 until 1865. While I was president, I led the United States through the **Civil War** (1861-1865). I helped to end slavery too. These are the accomplishments people most remember me for.

Abraham Lincoln was the sixteenth president of the United States.

Where and when were you born?

Abe says: I was born on a small farm in Kentucky in 1809. But my family moved to Indiana when I was around seven years old. There, my father built a small cabin and started a farm. My family worked very hard, but we didn't have much money.

When I was young, my mother died. Later, my father married a woman named Sarah. Sarah was smart and kind. She thought I was smart too! Sarah encouraged me to study and learn. She even let me read her books.

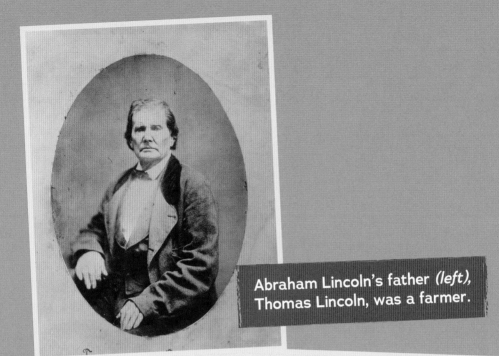

Abraham Lincoln's father *(left)*, Thomas Lincoln, was a farmer.

Abraham Lincoln's family lived in this cabin in Indiana.

What was your childhood like?

Abe says: I had to work very hard. Instead of going to school, I helped my father take care of the farm. But even though I spent my days farming, I still found time to read and learn. I kept a book in my pocket while I was plowing the fields. When the horses rested, I would stop and read. In the evening, after my work was done, I read books by the light of the fire.

Abraham Lincoln would often stop to rest and read while helping his father work.

What kinds of jobs did you have?

Abe says: When I grew up, I became a lawyer. That meant I could spend a lot of time reading, but I could spend time helping people too. I tried to make sure the law treated people fairly.

I also became a member of the Illinois House of Representatives. Later, I was elected to the United States Congress as well. I helped make new laws for my state and for our country. I also gave many speeches about my beliefs. I showed people that I had strong opinions and that I could speak up for myself.

This portrait shows Abraham Lincoln as a young lawyer.

Why did you want to be president?

Abe says: One reason I wanted to be president was to stop the spread of slavery. In some states, white people were allowed to own black people as slaves. Slaves had to work for their owners without pay.

In the 1850s, the United States was growing. The country was gaining more land and more states. Some people wanted to allow slavery in the new states. But I disagreed. I thought people should be treated fairly no matter the color of their skin. I didn't think any of our new states should allow slavery.

Abraham Lincoln addresses Knox College in Illinois during his 1858 Senate campaign. Lincoln told voters that slavery should not spread. He thought slavery was wrong.

How did people feel about your ideas?

Abe says: A lot of people in the northern states agreed with me. Slavery was already illegal, or against the law, in most northern states. Many northerners thought that slavery should not be allowed in the new states.

But many white people in the southern states did not like my plans. These people made a lot of money from the work of slaves. And they were worried that if I made slavery illegal in the new states, I would make slavery illegal in their states too. The southern states warned that if I was elected president, they would leave the United States.

Many slaves in southern states worked on cotton farms.

What happened next?

Abe says: I won the election. And many southern states kept their promise. During 1860 and 1861, eleven states **seceded** from the United States. That means they broke away. They formed their own country called the Confederate States of America.

I worried that if I let these southern states leave, the rest of the country would fall apart. I believed we could be strong only if all the states were united. So I decided to fight the Confederate states to keep the country together. I sent the United States Army, which was called the **Union** army, to fight the Confederate army. This started the Civil War.

Abraham Lincoln was sworn into office in Washington, DC, on March 4, 1861.

What happened during the Civil War?

Abe says: The two sides fought many battles. Homes and even cities were destroyed. Many people died. I felt terrible about this. But I kept working to keep our country together. I visited battlefields and kept track of what the armies were doing. If a general in my army wasn't doing his job well, I fired him. Then I tried to find a better general. I finally picked Ulysses S. Grant to lead the Union army. With Grant in charge, the Union started winning more battles.

This painting shows the Union's attack on Marye's Heights during the Battle of Fredericksburg in Virginia in December 1862.

Abe says: I gave many speeches. One of my most famous speeches is the **Gettysburg Address**. In my speech, I honored the people who had died in the war. I reminded people that the war was important. We were fighting for freedom and for our country. This gave people new hope.

I also wanted to find a way to end slavery. The Confederacy needed slaves to work for their army. Without slaves, the Confederacy would be much weaker. By ending slavery, I could do what I thought was right *and* help the Union fight the war.

Lincoln delivers the Gettysburg Address in Pennsylvania in 1863.

How did you try to end slavery?

Abe says: In 1863, I published a very important document: the **Emancipation** Proclamation. The proclamation said that slaves who lived in the Confederate states were now free.

The proclamation also let freed slaves join the Union army. These soldiers could fight for their own freedom. But the proclamation didn't make slavery illegal in the whole country. It made slavery illegal only in the Confederate states. The United States had to wait several more years before all the slaves were free.

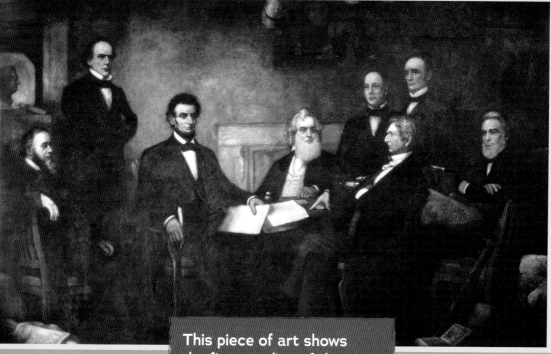

This piece of art shows
the first reading of the
Emancipation Proclamation.

When were all slaves freed?

Abe says: In 1865, Congress passed the Thirteenth **Amendment**. The amendment made slavery illegal in the United States. Passing the amendment had been hard work. Not everyone in Congress wanted slavery to end. But I worked to convince them that all people should be free.

That same year, the war ended too. On April 9, 1865, Confederate army general Robert E. Lee **surrendered** to General Grant. The Union had finally won the war.

Robert E. Lee surrenders at Appomattox Court House. His surrender marked the end of the Civil War.

What happened after the war?

Abe says: The country's troubles were not over. Many people in the South were angry that they had lost the war. Many cities and homes had been destroyed. And life was very hard for freed slaves. We had to spend a long time helping the country heal. This period was called **Reconstruction**.

I had many plans for Reconstruction. But only one week after the Civil War ended, I was killed by a man named John Wilkes Booth. I wasn't able to help the country through this difficult time. But others tried to continue the work I started.

The Lincoln Memorial is in Washington, DC. It was built to honor Abraham Lincoln.

How did America change because of you?

Abe says: I kept our country together through the Civil War. And I helped slaves become free. In our country today, people cannot be slaves, no matter what the color of their skin.

Timeline

1809   Abraham Lincoln is born in Kentucky.

1830   Abe leaves home and settles in Illinois.

1834   Abe is elected as representative to the Illinois state legislature.

1842   Abe marries Mary Todd.

1846   Abe is elected to the US Congress.

1860   Abe is elected president of the United States.

1861   The Civil War begins.

1863   Abe issues the Emancipation Proclamation.

1864   Abe is elected to a second term as president.

1865   The Civil War ends with a Union victory. Abe is shot and killed by John Wilkes Booth. And the Thirteenth Amendment officially becomes part of the Constitution.

Glossary

amendment: an official change to the United States Constitution

Civil War: the US war between the North and the South, which lasted from 1861 to 1865

emancipation: the process of freeing people who are slaves

Gettysburg Address: a famous speech given by Abraham Lincoln during the Civil War

Reconstruction: the time after the Civil War when people had to rebuild what had been destroyed in the war

seceded: officially broke apart from a group

surrendered: agreed to stop fighting and officially admitted the loss

Union: the states that did not secede from the United States in 1861

Further Information

Books

Barton, Jen. *What's Your Story, Harriet Tubman?* Minneapolis: Lerner Publications, 2016. Learn how Harriet Tubman helped people escape from slavery before the Civil War.

Stevenson, Augusta. *Abraham Lincoln.* New York: Aladdin, 2015. What was Abe like when he was a boy? This book explores the future president's childhood.

St. George, Judith. *Stand Tall, Abe Lincoln.* New York: Puffin, 2015. Abraham Lincoln became who he is partly because of his stepmother. Learn more about Sarah Bush Lincoln and her famous stepson in this book.

Websites

National Geographic Kids: Presidential Fun Facts
http://kids.nationalgeographic.com/content/kids/en_US
/explore/history/presidential-fun-facts
This kid-friendly website has some surprising facts about Abraham Lincoln.

US Presidents for Kids
http://kids.usa.gov/government/presidents/index.shtml
Learn about Lincoln and the other presidents on the federal government's special website for kids.

Index

Photo Acknowledgments

The images in this book are used with the permission of: © The Huntington Library/Bridgeman Images, p. 5; Library of Congress, pp. 7 (top), 17; © Liszt Collection/Bridgeman Images, p. 7 (bottom); © George Eastman House/Getty Images, p. 9; © Pictorial Press Ltd/Alamy, p. 11; AP Photo, p. 13; © Corbis, p. 15; ©Peter Newark Military Pictures/ Bridgeman Images, p. 19; © Private Collection/Bridgeman Images, p. 21; © Library of Congress/Bridgeman Images, p. 23; © National Geographic Creative/Bridgeman Images, p. 25; © Curved Light USA/Alamy, p. 27.

Front cover: Library of Congress.